THE UNIVERSAL COLLECTIVE UNCONSCIOUS

AND THE

METAPHYSICAL UTOPIA

THE UNIVERSAL COLLECTIVE UNCONSCIOUS
AND THE
METAPHYSICAL UTOPIA

By

Vincent J. Leardi

ISBN 1-58500-454-5

About the Book

The purpose of this book is to logically substantiate the existence of a Universal Collective Unconscious and its chaotic cycle of infinite and recurring change. The message of this book is that the human species should collectively seek to evolve to realize our part in the Universal Collective Unconscious (UCU). The UCU is the "First Cause" and the overriding continuous cause from which all evolution and devolution occur. The UCU is a continuous change of condition from which all abstract entities and physical matter continuously and chaotically change form while combining to make up the Cosmic Whole.

The term "Collective Unconscious" may also be interchangeable with the following terms; Chaotic Void, Universal Intelligence, Cosmos, Nature, Will, Eternal Stream of Unconscious, God-mind, Human Fnergy Field, Primal Energy, God, Infinite mind, Universal mind, Implicate Order, the Dialectical Whole, the Yin and the Yang and UCU. All of these terms are metaphors created to provide an expression for the Whole from which we, all species, matter and abstract entities come from, are part of and always will be a part of whether consciously or unconsciously. Language itself, which this thesis and all theses, idcas and human communication come from is merely the UCU expressing itself.

Humanity is the UCU or implicate universal mind realizing itself in its highest form of evolution.

Such a global realization of Collective Unconscious in the aforementioned context will provide the foundation for a metaphysical Global Society harmoniously and peacefully reflecting the Universal Whole we are part of and which we in fact are the summation of.

Throughout this thesis I will refer to a combination of disciplines to substantiate the existence of a Collective Unconscious and its manifestations. These disciplines include: Philosophy, Psychology, Religion, and Science (encompassing Physics, Cosmology, Biology & chemistry). The fact that there are common themes throughout all of these disciplines is in itself a statement of the Universal Whole of a guiding Collective Unconscious. These themes will be revealed and explained in the *book*.

Table of Contents

PART I

THE COLLECTIVE UNCONSCIOUS AND ITS INFINITE CHAOTIC CYCLE

PART II

THE METAPHYSICAL UTOPIA

PART I

THE COLLECTIVE UNCONSCIOUS AND ITS
INFINITE CHAOTIC CYCLE

Chapter 1 - Introduction: Defining the Collective Unconscious

The Psychoanalytic definition of the "Unconscious" is that it is the "…sum of all thoughts, memories, impulses, desires, feelings etc. of which the individual is not conscious but which influence his emotions and behavior…" This definition, developed by Dr. Sigmund Freud, refers to the individual Unconscious. Carl Jung, the famous Swiss psychiatrist and founder of 'Analytical Psychology' expanded the concept of the Unconscious to be Universal and Collective. Hence, we may define the "Collective Unconscious" as the sum of all thoughts, memories, impulses, desires, feelings, etc. which ever were and which always will be. This Collective Unconscious is the producer of all archetypal images. In other words, for the purposes of this thesis, the "Collective Unconscious" is every form of entity and event , both abstract and physical, that ever existed and ever will exist. It is infinite and recurring in a chaotic cycle of ever-changing events. It is the "First Cause" and the overriding continuous cause from which all evolution and devolution occur. The Collective Unconscious is a continuous change of condition from which all abstract entities and physical matter continuously and chaotically change form while combining to make up the Cosmic Whole.

The term "Collective Unconscious", for the purpose of this thesis, may also be interchangeable with the following terms; Chaotic Void, Universal Intelligence, Cosmos, Nature, Will, Eternal Stream of Unconscious, God-mind, Human Energy Field, Primal Energy, God, Infinite mind. All of these terms are metaphors created to provide an expression for the Whole from which we and all species, matter, and abstract terms come from, are part of, and will always be a part of whether consciously or unconsciously. Language itself, which this thesis and all theses, ideas and human communication come from, is merely the Collective Unconscious expressing itself. Humanity is the Collective Unconscious realizing itself in its highest form of evolution. The message of this thesis, is that the human species should collectively seek to evolve to realize our part in the Collective Unconscious. The purpose of this thesis is to logically substantiate the existence of the Collective Unconscious and its chaotic cycle of infinite and recurring change. Such a global realization of the Collective Unconscious in the aforementioned context will provide the foundation for a metaphysical Global Society harmoniously and peacefully reflecting the Universal Whole we are part of, embody, and which we in fact are the summation of.

Throughout this thesis I will refer to a combination of disciplines to substantiate the existence of a Collective Unconscious and its manifestations. These disciplines include: Philosophy, Psychology, Religion, and Science (encompassing Physics, Cosmology, Biology & Chemistry). The fact that there are common themes throughout all of these disciplines is in itself a statement of the Universal Whole of a guiding Collective Unconscious. These themes will be revealed and explained in the following chapters.

Chapter 2 - <u>The Dominance of the Cycle and Chaotic Linkage</u>

Examples of a Universal Collective Unconscious abound in Human History and even in

Pre-Historic times. Whether you ascribe to the Big Bang Theory or the Eternal Recurrence Theory, you cannot disprove an infinite cycle of Collective Unconscious dynamics. The Big Bang theory proposes that the Universe was created out of a dense singularity which exploded into an infinite expansion of matter. The Eternal Recurrence is "...An Ancient Cosmological idea, seized upon by the German Philosopher Friedrich Nietzsche, to the effect that everything that happens is part of an endlessly repeating cycle or sequence of events." [Honderich (1995:251)] Logically you can have both a single moment of creation, as in the Big Bang or the Biblical Genesis, and still espouse the Eternal Recurrence. You would just allow for the Big Bang to occur after the Universe either contracted back to a singular density via a series of Black Holes (voids in space which gravitationally pull all matter into it and absorb it.) This

can continuously happen in a chaotic cycle. Big Bang →
Infinite Expansion →Black Holes gradually pulling matter
into its Gravitational Void even in the midst of this
Expansion → Big Bang→etc.

Such a cycle does not deny the existence of God. Keep
in mind that the word God is a human metaphor that can be
interchangeable with other terms, one of them being the
Collective Unconscious. The Collective Unconscious,
Primal Energy, or God, which is every entity and event in
infinite time, can be said to be the primal condition of this
infinite cycle. Hence, we have just developed a logically
based scenario where a scientific idea (Big Bang), a
philosophical idea (Eternal Recurrence), and a Religious
belief in One God, can all coexist in the same theory. They
complement each other rather than contradict. This is the
concept of the Universal Whole of the Collective
Unconscious which cannot be disproved because it
encompasses every theory and thesis.

Every philosophical belief and thought, whether
fictional or tangent, exists. Some appear more physical
than others and some only exist in an abstract sense.
However, if it can be imagined only as a mind object, an
entity still exists as such. For example: A three eyed

monster may not be seen by the naked eye or touched by the human hand, but it can be projected in the mind so it nevertheless has an existence as a mind object.

Everything is abstract before it becomes concrete. A building is conceived of by the human mind and constructed mentally before it is physically built. Hence, everything that exists materialistically, organically, or inorganically first existed in the abstract chaos of the Collective Unconscious from which it will also eventually return to and change form. Essentially nothing is made or destroyed and nobody is born or dies. They just change form in the Collective Unconscious just as energy and matter changes form. $E=mc^2$ is Einstein's physical theory of Relativity put into the language of a mathematical equation. A metaphysical theory of Relativity could be expressed as U.C.U = Σ Entities meaning the Universal Collective Unconscious (U.C.U) equals and is interchangeable with the infinite Sum of All Entities. Remember, an entity can be any abstract idea, real or imagined, as well as any physical matter. U.C.U. is the Whole and Σ Entities is the summation of all of its parts. Every part, or Entity, contains the Whole within it. Nowhere is this concept of Metaphysical Relativity better depicted than in this passage from The Holographic Universe.

> "In a universe in which all things are infinitely interconnected, all consciousness are also interconnected. Despite appearances, we are all beings without borders. Or as Bohm put it, Deep down the consciousness of mankind is one."

Michael Talbot is referring here to the Holographic model and Implicate order concepts of the late theoretical physicist David Bohm, who was a protégé of Albert Einstein. Bohm's interconnected Consciousness make up Jung's Collective Unconscious.

The Collective Unconscious is the Implicate or enfolded order, the whole. Our existence and the existence of all separate entities is the explicate or unfolded order. We again refer to Talbot's appraisal of Bohm theory:

> "In his general theory of relativity Einstein astounded the world when he said that space and time are not separate entities ,

but are smoothly linked and part of a larger whole he called the space-time continuum. Bohm takes this idea a giant step further. He says that everything in the Universe is part of a continuum. Despite the apparent separateness of things at the explicate level, everything is a seamless extension of *everything* else, and ultimately even the implicate and explicate orders blend into each other."

Common themes in the Collective Unconscious are found in an endless cycle. Whether these themes are Philosophical, Religious, or Scientific, they all essentially say the same thing in different ways. They are archetypes, as Jung would say, or Forms, as Plato would say, repeated over and over abstractly and manifested physically.

Starting with Philosophy we see correlation between Eastern and Western philosophers. The idea of Continuous Flux was espoused by Buddha as well as by the Pre-Socratic Greek philosopher Heraclitus. The Cosmological concept of the eternal recurrence was part of the Ancient Egyptian and Hindu beliefs and was later adopted by the famous 19th Century German philosopher Friedrich Nietzsche. The Big Bang/Big-Crunch theory on the Universe is a modern scientific theory developed in the 20th century. This theory of a continuously expanding and contracting Universe reflects the cyclical pattern of an eternal recurrence. The Void in Buddhism and Hinduism is the concept of the whole from which we and all matter are a part of, originate from and return to, in a continuous cycle. This belief is also reflected in the Christian Bible, in Genesis referring to the Void being prevalent at the beginning of creation. A modern Scientific Theory called Vacuum Genesis claims that the Big Bang originated from the primordial chaos of the Void. All throughout nature, history, and in our daily lives we see the archetype of the cycle. Some examples;

Day→Night

Breakfast→Lunch→Dinner

Birth→Life→Death

Winter→Spring→Summer→Fall

Days of the Week

Months of the Year

Wake→Sleep→Wake

All of these examples reflect the pattern of a continuos recurring cycle. At the Universal Level Energy moves towards entropy or increasing disorder. This is occurring as the Universe expands. However the Big Bang and other theories as well as Religious and Philosophical beliefs propose that orderly matter as we know it originated from the Primordial Chaos. Hence we can make an argument for the following Universal Cycles;

Chaos→Order→Chaos

Unconscious Will→Conscious Intellect→Unconscious Will

Void→Matter→Void

Entropy→Energy→Entropy

Dispersion/Diversity→Singularity/Unity→Dispersion/Diversity

These physical cycles correspond to abstract cycles inherent in many Religious beliefs and Philosophical ideas. While the mundane cycles of our physical world are orderly and predictable, the Abstract and even physical cycles of the Universe and the Collective Unconscious are chaotic.

For example, while the Universe is still expanding creating more *entropy* and invisible space known as Dark Matter, Black Holes are simultaneously pulling matter into an infinite density moving towards *Singularity*. The cycles of metaphysical and scientific theories throughout Human History are also chaotic and erratic. Science and Philosophy has at one time or another espoused theories and theses that have supported Religious beliefs in One God creating all, as is the case with the Big Bang Singularity or the Pre-Renaissance concepts of the Earth being the center of the Universe. At other times Science and Philosophy has been at odds with religion as was the case with Galileo and Darwin. However, in every case we can see a cycle of the opposites. That is that every thesis has an anti-thesis. Every idea, without fail, has an opposing idea, every belief a counter belief. At different times a belief or theory will prevail only to be disproved and replaced in the future by a theory that although new, is still composed of the same archetype or form as a previous theory in the past. If no thesis or theory can even be permanently prevailing and without dispute, we must conclude that all theories, ideas, forms and archetypes are all true at one time or another in repetitive but not sequential cycles in infinite time. All of these Archetypes or forms make up the Collective Unconscious.

The thesis - antithesis concept itself is a common theme shared among different philosophers at different times in history. This Dialectic concept was used by Socrates and Plato and it was applied to arguments by Immanual Kant to show that principles of Science have contradictory aspects. The famous 19th Century philosopher George Wilhelm Friedrich Hegel "… thought that all logic and world history itself followed a dialectical path in which internal contradictions were transcended but gave rise to new contradictions that themselves required resolution."

Evolution is another cycle that is constant, infinite and chaotic. Although we all as humans evolve from the basic cosmic elements, after we die we may devolve to a different life form or an inorganic life form. We may also reincarnate but that would not classify as progressively evolving since we would take on the same form with either less or more intellectual capacity. In other words, evolution is not always one species advancing to another superior species. It is the cyclical amalgamation of organic and inorganic elements in no particular order creating life in its varying forms (plant, animal, vegetable) or abstract entities all of which are part of and reside in the Collective Unconscious. The evolutionist John Maynard Smith presents a strong argument for random and chaotic nature of evolution in the following statement:

> "If one was able to replay the whole evolution of animals, starting at the bottom of the Cambrian (and, to satisfy Laplace, moving one of the individual animals two feet to its left), thereis no guarantee indeed, no likelihood - that the result would be the same. There might be no conquest of the lands, no emergence of mammals, certainly no human beings."The famous mathematical physicist Roger Penrose also attests to the chance-like, chaotic nature of evolution when he states that…

> "Things at least seem to organize themselves somewhat better than they ought to, just on the basis of blind-chance evolution and natural selection."

Penrose cites the fact that the algorithms of the human mind and of human DNA are both created by "blind - chance evolution and natural selection."

In other words, a bundle of chaotic conditions merged randomly to produce different species of life to include the human species. These conditions all exist in the Collective Unconscious and in their chaotic cycle cause different effects. We are only one of these effects that combine to make up the Cosmic Whole. This lends us to describe the Universe in terms of a chaotic Determinism. Chaotic in that events and entities are in constantly changing in a random sequence. The Universe is Deterministic to the extent that although events occur randomly they do change *constantly*. One thing is for certain and that is change. This is affirmed by the philosophies of Buddha, Heraclitus and the Hindus. The Universe is also Deterministic because the same events occur over and over again in a recurring cycle. However when and in what manner these events occur varies, lending to the chaotic nature of occurrences. Chaotic Determinism is best described by the definition of "Chaos Theory" listed in the Oxford Companion to Philosophy. "Chaos Theory" is defined in this reference book as:

"The theory of apparently *random* behavior within a *deterministic* system such as weather. The unpredictability of a chaotic system is not due to any lack of governing laws but to the outcome being sensitive to minute, unmeasurable variations in the initial conditions. An example is the 'butterfly effect': the idea that the mere flap if a butterfly's wing can make the difference between a hurricane occurring and not occurring.

The term chaotic - determinism also exhibits the holistic nature if the Universe. It is a paradoxical concept that includes every possibility which means that for the purposes of this thesis it defines the nature of the Collective Unconscious. The nature of the Universal Collective Unconscious is dialectic in that it moves from thesis to antithesis to synthesis. The dialectic movement here is from Chaos to Determinism to the collective Chaotic-Determinism where we have an eternal recurring cycle of causes and effects randomly occurring. The fact that we can use this argument to support the dialectic and holistic nature of the Collective Unconscious means that we can put Hegel, Plato, Buddha, the Hindus, Nietzsche, Bohm and many other conjectures in the same camp where before they were seen as having diverse views. Plato, Buddha, Nietzsche and the Hindus all espouse the eternal cyclical nature of things while Hegel sponsored a dialectic view of the world in a holistic fashion. The holistic aspect of Hegel's Dialectic movement is in line with David Bohm's Implicate order.

Now that we have documented some examples of the chaotic cyclical nature of the Collective Unconscious, let us add a few more examples of documentation supporting the existence the Collective Unconscious. One such example we have just mentioned: the commonality of philosophical concepts from people not normally put in the same camp of thought. Earlier in this chapter, I showed examples of commonality among Scientific, Religious and Philosophical ideas. The Libet experiment conducted by neurophychologists Benjamin Libet and Bernard Feinstein is yet more evidence to support a case for a Universal Collective Unconscious. The experiment and its results were as follows:

" Libet and Feinstein measured the time it took for a touch stimulus on a patient's skin to reach the brain as an electrical signal. The patient was also asked to push a button when he or she became aware of being touched. Libet and Feinstein found that the brain registered the stimulus in 0.0001 of second after it occurred, and the patient pressed the button 0.1 of a second after the stimulus was applied. But remarkably, the patient didn't report being consciously aware of either stimulus or pressing the button for almost 0.5 seconds. This meant that the decision to respond was being made by the patient's unconscious mind.....

Even more disturbing, none of the patients Libet and Feinstein tested were aware that their unconscious minds had already caused them to push the button before they had consciously decided to do so....This has caused some researchers to wonder if free will is an illusion." [Talbot (1991:191-192)]

If free will is the illusion than the Collective Unconscious is the reality.

Another experiment conducted by Valerie Hunt, professor of Kinesiology at UCLA, also lends substance to the existence and prevalence of the Universal Collective Unconscious.   Hunt developed a way to confirm experimentally the existence of the human energy field. This human energy field for purposes of this thesis can be interchangeable with the term Collective Unconscious. (Remember words are archetypes of the Collective Unconscious expressing itself.)   In her experiment Hunt used 2 devices; an Electroencephalograph to make Electroencephalograms (EEGs) of the brains electrical activity and an electromyograph (which measures electrical activity of human muscles) to make electromyograms (EMGs) of a human energy field.   Hunt discovered that the human energy field responds to stimuli even before the brain does. The experiment and its results;

"She has taken EMG readings of the energy field and EEG readings of the brain simultaneously and discovered that when she makes a loud sound or flashes a bright light, the EMG of the energy field registers the stimulus before it ever shows up on the EEG.

The discovery led Hunt to conclude that the brain is just a real sophisticated computer and that "mind" is not in the brain but in the energy field.

If the brain is a computer then the "Collective Unconscious" or " Infinite Mind" is one with the Human Energy field and is the "Input" to the Computer. The electrical impulses in the brain are interconnected with the energy in the field. Electrochemical elements in the brain and throughout the rest of the human body are linked and united to electrochemical elements in the Cosmos. We evolved form the Cosmos and are made of elements from the Cosmos. Another example of the interrelationship of everything culminating in the human mind which collectively reflects the Cosmos it evolved from and which it is part of. Recall from chapter one, that Cosmos, human energy field, and infinite mind, are all terms interchangeable with the Universal Collective Unconscious.

It is interesting to note here that the ancient Hindus' literature indicated a belief in a human vibrational field which linked us to the Cosmos. Again, we see a recurring idea or archetype from the Collective Unconscious occurring to define the Collective Unconscious itself. The ancient beliefs and scientific experiments are linked via the Universal archetype of the Human Energy, or Vibration Field.

Finally, one last note about the Hunt experiment is that the higher frequencies in the EEG and EMG readings produced chaotic patterns with random changes. Another testament to the chaotic whole that is the Collective Unconscious.

Chapter 3 - <u>Correlations in Thought and Experience</u>

In the previous chapter, we reviewed literature (Philosophical, Religious, and Scientific) and some actual documented experiments that substantiated the existence of a Universal Collective Unconscious and its cyclical chaotic nature. In this chapter, we will explore everyday human and objective experiences which have been prevalent throughout history and are on-going and continuing. We will also use *common sense logic* to further substantiate the Collective Unconscious and its infinite chaotic cycle.

First, let us look at the common experiences, instincts and desires shared among the human species and other forms of life. In chapter 2, we referred to Cosmic evolution as the reason for our existence. This cosmic evolution is an endless chaotic cycle, an amalgamation of conditions. The conditions of a Primordial Chaos, which is described by Buddha, the Hindus and the Christian Bible's Genesis as

"The Void," formed matter. Most of matter is "Dark Matter" invisible to visual or radio detection. About 1% of the matter in the Universe is detectable and forms all the physical manifestations, such as galaxies, stars and planets, etc. Earth, of course, is only one of these planets which formed about five billion years ago. Throughout this 5 billion year history the Cosmic elements i.e. Oxygen, Hydrogen, Carbon, and many others formed the foundations for organic life. Plants formed under water, certain plants evolved into fish. Fish evolved into reptiles. Reptiles evolved into mammals and later primates. Man, only within the last million years or so, evolved as the most sophisticated form of primate. Modern man evolved over the last 10,000 years from Homo-erectus, Cro-Magnon and Homo-sapien species. The first obvious commonality that Humans have with all of the species and elements aforementioned is that they all evolved from a previous form and originated from the Primordial Chaos or Void. When all of these life forms die they all go back to the Primordial Chaos, Void or Collective Unconscious and change form again.

While we evolve, we still retain elements and characteristics from the other organic and inorganic forms which all combine to make one chaotic cycle of entities referred to in this thesis as the Collective Unconscious. Some examples of cross species linkage include the desires and instincts for survival, reproduction, and territoriality. These traits are common in all living sentient beings and species. Reptiles, Fish, Mammals and Humans all eat, sleep, consume and require air and water. Even plants require air and water to live. The chemical compounds and elements in the atmosphere and in the far reaches of the Universe are contained in human bodies and those of other living creatures. This is why drugs, alcohol, or any other chemical substance has such an impact on our minds and bodies. We are all biochemical and electrochemical units extremely sensitive to outside chemical substances which alter our toxic composite. Here again is an example of our evolution from Cosmic sources, in this case, Cosmic chemical sources, to our present state. Our sensitivity and addictiveness to chemicals indicate that we are part of and one with this Cosmic Alchemy.

Electricity is another Cosmic source that impacts substantially on our brain, mind, and body. As we saw in the Hunt experiment in chapter 2, electricity links our brain and bodies to the Cosmic Primal Energy. If you recall the

Hunt experiment demonstrated how we were one and the same with this Cosmic Primal Energy, Human Energy Field or Universal Collective Unconscious. Further examples of our link to electricity is the use of electro-shock treatment or electro-cardio resuscitation to revive the heart and stimulate the brain.

As we mentioned earlier in chapters 1 and 2, evolution is not progressive but cyclical and chaotic. We are just as capable as devolving as we are of evolving. People who are born with mental deficiencies, due to genetic or chemical imbalances reflect a type of the devolution. We can make the analogy that a person either born with or develops mental retardation, depression or other mental diseases is devolving toward a vegetative state more in line with the Consciousness of a plant than with a human. Of course, there are chemicals that can bring the person out of a catatonic or vegetative state. In some cases chemical drugs can even improve the mental acuteness of retarded people. Contrarily, drugs, alcohol and other chemical substances can throw a person into a coma, catatonic or vegetative state. Hence, we see that chemical compounds can either help us evolve or cause us to devolve attesting to the chaotic nature of evolution.

Another example of devolution is the human propensity for war and territoriality. Here again, the human and spirit regresses to seek territory as symbol of power. Territory is also sought by governments out of greed or fear. These instincts are the same as those of reptiles and predatory mammals. The will to power and the instinct to fear are archetypes of the Collective Unconscious common in all living species and sentient beings. We see the cyclical recurring nature of these archetypes in the pre-historic times of the first living organism to the history of wars and violence that have plagued mankind right up the present day.

This cycle is again chaotic because intermixed with the primitive violence, man has also evolved to great spiritual and intellectual heights of progress. Some of these include; our exploration of the Universe, technological advances, and medical advances which enable us to prolong life. Unfortunately and paradoxically many of these technological, scientific and medical advances develop and spring out of a war-time environment.

Now, to the subject of infinity or eternity. Remember the cycle of the Collective Unconscious is eternally and infinitely recurring. The first substantiation of eternity is that we can conceive of it as an abstract concept. We do this in our religious doctrines as well as our scientific and philosophical theories. The theory of an expanding Universe is supported by Hubble's discovery of a Red-Shift change in the telescopic spectrum which indicates that galaxies are moving away from each other and expanding. Christian, Judiac and Islamic religions speak of One God who always was and always will be. God is portrayed as eternal and everlasting. In Chapter 2, we spoke of the eternal recurrence philosophies of the Hindus, Buddha, Plato and Nietzsche.

Another example which supports the infinity concept involves the correlation of scientific theory and human experience. Earlier we stated that the human body and human brain were electro-chemical units. Electro-magnetic forces are scientifically known to be infinite in range. Hence, we have a linkage in our anatomy with an infinite force, electricity.

Light is carried by photons whose range is also infinite. The majority of people who have had near death experiences (NDE) state that they entered "...A realm composed of light, higher vibrations or frequencies." Before being revived, NDEers "...frequently say that the realm is suffused with a light more brilliant than any they have ever seen on earth..."

NDEers indicate that they not only see light, but are actually part of the bright light and the vibrations or frequencies. This is becoming part of and one with the Infinite Chaotic Whole I have been referring to as the Collective Unconscious. In the case of NDEs we become part of light and electromagnetic frequencies which are both infinite in range. Hence we become one with infinity.

Dreams also enable us to enter the realm of the chaotic Collective Unconscious. Many times our dreams are a chaotic mixture of desires and fears. Our dreams are often not in any order and with no sense or purpose. Another example of the chaotic nature of the Collective Unconscious. Near Death experiences and dreams are two common experiences human beings engage in unconsciously. They are our empirical entry into infinity, chaos and the Collective Unconscious. They are also the height of our awareness as being part of the Infinite Chaotic whole that is the Collective Unconscious.

Now to some common sense logic. We explored some examples of cycles in chapter 2. More examples of cycles include: the cyclical nature of human inventions such as the washer/dryer, clocks and the wheel. This and many other examples substantiate the cycle as a dominant archetype in the Collective Unconsciousness and attests to the existence of time as an eternal cycle of events.

Another point of logic is to relate the concept of cause and effect to the existence of A-priori knowledge. A-priori knowledge is knowledge and concepts which exist abstractly independent of sensory experience. The existence of A-priori knowledge is acknowledged by one of the greatest theoretical and empirical scientists, Albert Einstein. Einstein's perspective on A-priori knowledge is summed up in this paragraph from <u>Albert Einstein: Philosopher-Scientist</u>:

> "According to Einstein, the concepts which arise in thought and in our Linguistic expression are free creations of thought which cannot be derived inductively from sensory experiences.
>
> Like Plato, Einstein stresses the gap between data of sense and concepts of thought. He contends that there is a gulf, logically unbridgeable, which separates the world of sensory 'experiences from the

realm of concepts' and conceptual relations which constitute prepositions. The constructive nature of concepts is not easily noticed, Einstein asserts, because we have the habit of combining certain concepts and conceptual relations definitively with certain sensory experiences."

If we believe in the existence of A-priori knowledge, and also acknowledge the external cycle of cause and effect, then the only logical *cause* for A-priori knowledge is the Collective Unconscious. The physics of cause and effect, and the theoretical logic of acknowledging A-priori knowledge combine to substantiate the metaphysical concept of the Collective Unconscious. Here again, is Hegel's Dialectical progression of the thesis (empirical cause and effect) and its antithesis (A-priori theory) to combine to form the metaphysical synthesis (The Universal Collective Unconscious).

Speaking of Hegel's dialectic, we see another correlation between a Western philosophy and an Eastern one. The Dialectic, as we discussed in chapter 2, has been supported by some very famous philosophers i.e., Socrates,

Plato, Kant and Hegel. The dialectic concept of every thesis having the seed of its antithesis in it, is similar to the ancient Chinese cosmological philosophy of the Yin and Yang.

> "The Yin-Yang school was interested in cosmology and portrayed the operation of the world as involving the interplay between two forces or elements, Yin, which is negative, passive, weak, and Yang, which is positive, active, and strong."

The Yin and Yang makes the Yin-Yang just like the thesis and antithesis make the synthesis. Another teaching of the ancient Yin-Yang philosophy is that the natural order of things operate in a cyclical fashion. The Yin-Yang school cites the change of seasons and the political changes in history as examples of this eternal cycle. The very symbol of the Yin-Yang illustrates an eternal cycle of Dialectic opposites.

The Yin-Yang philosophy, with its teaching of the interplay of weak and strong forces, is analogous to modern physical theories involving the interplay of strong and weak forces to make up the nucleus of the atom.

So in the ancient Chinese school of Yin-Yang philosophy, we see the recurring cycle of ancient and modern cosmological ideas, (Dialectical and cyclical philosophies). The ancient cosmological Hindu philosophies promoted the eternal recurring cycle, just as the ancient Yin-Yang philosophy, Buddha, Plato and Nietzsche. The dialectic of Plato, Socrates, Kant and Hegel match up with the paradox of the Yin-Yang philosophy.

Finally, if you recall in chapter 2, the "chaos theory" promotes a dialectic cycle of chaotic-determinism or chaos within order. This links Yin-Yang with the "Chaos Theory."

We have just illustrated how the ancient Yin-Yang philosophy substantiates the existence of a Chaotic Infinite Cycle of the Universal Collective Unconscious. The Yin-Yang philosophy ties together Chaos, Dialecticism and the Eternal recurring cycle. Another testament to the Holistic nature of the interconnected Cosmos or Collective Unconscious.

One last method worth mentioning before moving on to chapter 4, is the concept of "Linguistic Relativity." In chapter 2, we reviewed Einstein's physical theory of relativity ($E=mc^2$), my metaphysical theory of Relativity (U.C.U.=Σ Entities) and now we must mention the fact that all of our expressions; mathematical, literary, symbolic and spoken, are all forms of language. Language is the glue that synthesizes all our abstract thoughts and this thesis. The same ideas of language recur over and over again, and are just expressed differently by different manifestation of language. Pictures or symbols evolved into words and mathematical expressions only to devolve back into pornographic and violent cinema. Linguistic expressions follows the same chaotic infinite cycle as everything else we have mentioned in this thesis which substantiates the Universal Collective Unconscious. It is, as we said in chapter 1, the Collective Unconscious expressing itself.

Chapter 4 - <u>Linguistic Relativity and the Dominance of the Abstract</u>

Our first finding will be the last method mentioned in chapter 3, "Linguistic Relativity." If language is the Universal Collective Unconscious expressing itself, it is obviously our most important finding. Language leads us to the source of our being. We define Language in this thesis as any expression of the Collective Unconscious or any of its abstract and physical entities. It is the communicative link between all entities or parts of the Whole or Universal Collective Unconscious. Examples of language include pictures, symbols, signals, physical, writing, speech, words, music, cinema, literature, art and mathematics, etc. Every subject and discipline is an amalgamation of words which combine to form categories within Language. Such subjects and discipline include: Science, Philosophy, Religion, Entertainment, Art, Psychology, Anthropology, Geology, Cosmology, Social

Studies, Economics, etc. Every species has its own language form of communication. Humanity is the culmination of the Cosmic evolution and of every entity in the cosmos. Humanity and its communicative expressions are the expression of every entity. Everything we conceptualize must be expressed in some kind of language including this thesis. All theories, including Physical and metaphysical Relativity, are relative to Linguistic expression, (Linguistic Relativity). Language is the main common theme throughout our human history and it is also the only way of documenting Universal History and its future. It is the expression of everything, and so it is relative to every entity. Language is the Cosmos expressing itself as an implicate, holistic, chaotic and infinite recurring cycle, and is itself holistic, chaotic, infinite and recurring. I can only relate this thesis of the Universal Collective Unconscious with language, so I must conclude that the culmination of my existence is my ability to express my thesis through language. Language is everything because it is the only way we can express everything.

Language is also an A-priori entity. It exists with no physical cause other than that of a prevailing Universal Collective Unconscious or Cosmic mind. However, we can also say that language is A-posteriori due to the fact that it could not exist without the experience of sentient beings. Hence, language, the expression of the Collective Unconscious, is itself holistic, and dialectic, a thesis and antithesis within itself.

Any A-priori concept or general A-priori knowledge, i.e. language, substantiates a Universal Collective Unconscious. An anthropocentric view argues that anything we conceive of including this thesis and the concept of a Collective Unconscious is relative and restricted to our fleshy bodies and sensory perception. While this is true, as all theses and views are anthropocentric is an A-priori concept and a linguistic expression lending itself to being a manifestation of the Whole Cosmic Universal Collective Unconscious.

Mythology and Imagination are also A-priori effects which find their cause in the Collective Unconscious. As with language, and as part of language, mythology and imaginative ideas have their roots and causation in the Collective Unconscious. Their is no other logical, physical, philosophical, or neurobiological way to explain the existence of such A-priori phenomena as mythology, imagination or language. Only a metaphysical theory of the

Universal Collective Unconscious, the linguistic expression of this thesis.

Another crucial finding this thesis produced was cited earlier in chapter 2. That is, that no thesis, theory or belief is ever permanently prevailing. Hence nothing can be classified as untrue or non-existent. The only thing that is permanent is that conditions are always changing in an infinite recurring chaotic cycle. Every entity or thing that can be abstractly conceptualized or physically manifested exists in an eternal continuous flux. The Collective Unconscious is this continuous flux, the chaotic cause, and the "First Cause", that always was and will be the dominant and all encompassing *condition* from which all effects arise and become causes themselves. We can see the dominance of the abstract in our Universe. The more abstract, the more prevalent. Dark matter, which supposedly constitutes about 99% of the physical universe, is undetectable by radio or visual devices. Yet it is the main guiding gravitational force of all the galaxies and physical matter. Dark matter is the most abstract form of matter and is more abundant in quantity and force than any other physical form. Abstract ideas, intuition, instincts, and beliefs control the structure of our lives more than any other physical entity. Religious philosophy, theoretical science, morality, primal instincts, intuition, desires, emotions, psychological needs and cravings, and obsessions guide all of our decisions and actions. All of these common abstractions make up the Whole that is the Collective Unconscious otherwise known as the Universal Intelligence, Chaotic Void, Will, Infinite mind, Cosmos or God.

This Universal Collective Unconscious operates in a chaotic infinite recurring cycle. The fragmentation in our global society reflects this chaos and our quest to discover a unified theory of the Universe as well as beliefs in One God reflect the *Will* towards unity and singularity humanity seeks as leading representatives of the Universal Collective Unconscious. The simultaneous movement of humanity towards unity, and the physical universe towards chaotic entropy, exemplifies a chaotic-determinism that is cyclical and never ending. Another simultaneous movement is physical matter expanding infinitely, as evidenced by Hubble's red shift, and black holes pulling matter into singularity.

The literary, experimental, methodological, and empirical discussions in chapter 2 and 3 abound with examples that support and substantiate the finding of an all encompassing, implicate Universal Collective Unconscious, interchangeable with many other terms mentioned previously in this thesis describing One Cosmic Whole composed of everything or *All Entities*. The same language is used to describe different concepts which all say the same thing in a chaotic, random cycle of historical events, philosophical ideas, scientific theories and religious beliefs recurring over and over again. We have no evidence of a beginning or and end to this recurring cycle, so we must logically deduce it to be infinite and eternal. This deduction of infinity and eternity is supported by the greatest empirical and theoretical minds including the great Albert Einstein. Einstein supported a physical theory of relativity that saw all physical matter, time, and space as an infinite four dimensional continuum (three dimensions space & one dimension time). This thesis supports a *metaphysical eternal continuum* of infinite cyclical time with an infinite number of entities of which Einstein's physical relativity theory, all abstract theories, and physical matter are a part of. This Metaphysical Eternal Continuum is what I am calling the Universal Collective Unconscious.

Chapter 5 - <u>Some Practical Applications</u>

Now that we have substantiated our Finding of a Universal Collective Unconscious, we need to discuss how to apply this metaphysical concept to our global society.

The present day world is fragmented into different countries, ideologies, languages and religions. This is chaos acting in orderly matter or in this case orderly civilization. It is the dialectic and the Yin-Yang all over again. Out so-called Civilized society still contains the seed of the opposite, chaos, from which everything originates. This chaos is natural and can be healthy. However, all too often it breeds violence, prejudice, greed, misery and poverty. People become prejudice of each other's beliefs, color, and creed. Fear makes us suspicious of our neighbors at every level causing violence. Territoriality causes massive wars of destruction among nations. Greed causes humans to indulge in excesses at the expense of others.

Diversity in beliefs and views are part of nature and the Universal Collective Unconscious. However, it must be balanced with the will and desire for unity and singularity. Entropy must be balanced with unifying energy. This is the beauty of a metaphysical society. In a metaphysical society all beliefs are tolerated, and resources are allocated so that every human being can have a decent quality of life. Distribution of Energy needs, such as heat, air-conditioning and petroleum, would ensure every person the comforts necessary to combat the weather elements. Redistribution of food and water so that all people have adequate levels for comfortable existence is also a must. Finally, adequate housing should be provided for everyone. All of this can be accomplished within a democratic and even a capitalistic society. A large part of this is already being accomplished through governmental and civic organizations at every level. However, we as individuals need to collectively participate in our communities to supplement the governments efforts to clothe and feed the poor, house the homeless, and redistribute essential energy resources. All of these efforts would in itself help to reduce violence and crime. It would also reduce the amount of stress we collectively share.

Poverty, violence, obsessive competition, greed, avarice, economic and social stress, and our penchant for self-aggrandizement, are all obstacles that prevent us from realizing our part in the Cosmic Whole or Universal Collective Unconscious. These obstacles obstruct our ability to reach the height of our awareness, both individually and collectively. If One part of our global or Universal society is suffering, we all suffer a little because we are all interconnected.

So while our government, institutions, and charitable organizations, endeavor to cure some of these social ills, we must also all participate in our own small communities in whatever fashion we can to remove these obstacles to collective and individual awareness. Such community involvement would free up funds for our local and federal governments to improve conditions nationally and internationally.

The United States can serve as a Global and Universal model with numerous Metaphysical Communities functioning within our current Democratic structure. A perfect example of such a community is the Hopi Indian societies of Northern Arizona. N.J. Berrill describes the Hopi community in man's emerging mind:

"Public opinion is powerful and inescapable, leaders and people are closely associated, decisions are usually made by unanimous consent, and every individual is responsible for the welfare of the whole. Privilege does not exist, all thought and culture are directed toward the ideal of peace; religious tradition functions as the constitution, and all Hopi institutions express faith in a harmonious universe in which nature, man, and all living things, are mutually interdependent, bound together for the benefit of all. Leadership is unsought and is burdened with heavy moral responsibility. All in all the community is like the crew of a ship in a storm, bound together by the goal of survival with every soul in its place. The analogy is close, for as in the ship any betrayal of the common purpose may be disastrous when there is no margin for error, which has been the Hopi lot. And against this we see the wider world of man as a compounded confusion of purpose, uncertainty of method, and multiplicity of voice, desperately in need of direction."

If the Hopi society can collectively live in peace and harmony, certainly we in our respective communities; with substantially more resources, can do like-wise. We can substantially reduce crime, poverty, and misery, if we collectively combine resources and abilities in small manageable communal groups. This can be accomplished while still retaining all of our modern comforts and conveniences. Many small groups of interdependent communities would also reduce economic stress on many people. Once this occurs, everybody can focus on evolving themselves into an intellectual and spiritual awareness of their link to the Universal Collective Unconscious.

Democracy and capitalism need not be disturbed to accomplish this. If an individual wishes to work harder for more luxuries, so be it, as long as it is not at the expense of others. Every individual should have the quality of life, free of misery, poverty, and stress, so they can evolve and be in a state of mind to propose and formulate their own Metaphysical or Ontological thesis. When we all are in a state of mind to do this, we can collectively evolve and perhaps have a collective metaphysical thesis where everyone participates. Then we will all be consciously of one mind with the Cosmos or Universal Collective Unconscious. We will have bridged the gap Einstein and Plato speak of between sense data and concept of thought. The senses and concepts will be as one.

Chapter 6 - <u>Summarizing the U.C.U.</u>

Let us summarize our conclusions. Every entity exists, either abstractly or physically, interrelated with every other entity. All of these entities combine to formulate the U.C.U. (Universal Collective Unconscious) or Cosmos. The Cosmos is One, holistic entity, enfolded. All physical matter, including our existence, is the Cosmos or U.C.U. unfolded. All entities evolve and devolve from and into a Primordial Chaos or Void. This occurs in a random, chaotic and eternal cycle. There is no set sequence, purpose, or order to this cycle. There is only the existence of everything in a constant, infinite and chaotic flux.

The human species is the only known universal entity that can reach a level of awareness of itself as part of and one with the Universal Collective Unconscious. Humans devolve into other entities and forms before, during, and after their existence. Dreams and near death experiences are the two closest common experiences humans share as being part of the Primordial Chaos of the U.C.U. These are unconscious experiences.

We will reach the height of our evolution when we can collectively and *consciously* realize that we are part of and the summation of the Cosmos, Universal Collective Unconscious, Primal Energy, Void, Will, nature, or *God*. Then we will have a Universal Metaphysical Society composed of many small Metaphysical Communities. In this environment every human can use the universal archetype known as language to formulate his and her own thesis which can all be combined to formulate a Synthesis. This is our challenge and our destiny. As the old saying goes, "United we stand, divided we fall." Once fully united as one in mind and awareness we can finally "come full circle." Another one of an infinite number of abstract concepts which make up and express the Eternal recurring cycle of One Universal Collective Unconscious.

PART II

THE METAPHYSICAL UTOPIA

Chapter 7 - <u>Chaos and the Cosmos</u>

Before we embark upon creating our Utopian Society we must understand the ontology and metaphysics of Chaos and the Cosmos.

To understand Chaos and the Cosmos is to understand the entire eternal history and future of our being and the being of the whole Universe. It is to understand that we are already one with our origins and destiny. Actually the origin and destiny of our species, all of nature and the Universe is one holistic and Chaotic Entity. Time is cyclical and not linear. There is no beginning and no end. There is just a recurring chaotic infinite cycle of entities and events which are all part of and the summation of a Universal Intelligence or Universal Collective Unconscious. There is no actual past, present and future. There is only the abstract archetypes of fragmentation and categorization caused by chaos. Chaos causes the Human Species (the Summation of the Collective Unconsciousness) to fragment the holistic Entity of the

51

Universe into categories such as space-time, past, present, future, beginning and end.

The Cosmos is part of and one with the all dominant, prevalent and abstract chaos. That is why any attempt at Unity, whether in our Earthly Civilization or in our physical Universe, will always be disrupted and overtaken by Chaos. Has it not been established even by Cosmological and physical laws that the Universe and everything in it is constantly moving towards a state of entropy? Does not every endeavor of a nation or even the World to Unite in peace and harmony always become disrupted by war, revolution, greed, pride and the will to power? Entropy, war, greed, pride, and the will to power all have one thing in common, Chaos. They are all abstract forces that dominant our world and the Universe. The most abstract physical force or the most physical abstract force currently known to us is dark matter. More than 99% of the Universe is made up of this invisible gravitational force which controls the destiny of all physical entities to include all stars, galaxies, suns and planets. Hence, chaos is abstract and abstract is all prevalent, from the physical to the metaphysical. Dark matter is the dominant physical chaotic abstract and the Collective Unconscious or Universal

Intelligence is the dominant metaphysical chaotic abstract, and the ultimate dominating abstract which contains all entities and is within all entities. This ultimate dominating and all encompassing abstract is also called: God, Cosmic Mind, Chaotic Void, Void, Implicate order, Geist, Will, Tao, or Nature.

Every entity, to include abstract ideas, music, art, imagination, creativity, as well as all physical entities always existed and always will exist. For example: Although the airplane was invented in the 20th Century, Aristotle thought of the concept of an airplane around 400 B.C. Hence the airplane already existed as an abstract concept in the Universal Collective Unconscious long before it became a physical reality. Today's abstract fiction is tomorrow's physical reality. We see this time and time again. Great writers often prophesize future developments in their abstract fiction. Fiction, imagination and mythology are A-priori abstractions that complement physical developments because in the Implicate order of things, they are actually one with these physical manifestations. Fiction and reality, sense perception and concept of thought are more examples of fragmentation and categorization spawned from Chaos.

In the reality of the Implicate Order Fiction is one with Reality, Sense perception is one with Concept of thought, Chaos is one with the Cosmos, origin is one with destiny. The Chaotic Void is the all encompassing abstract entropy containing all that ever was before we see it as reality. The dominance of Chaos conditions us to perceive the Implicate Order in Explicate, fragmentary terms.

We may take heart in the fact that the Implicate order enfolded in Chaos means that nothing including our Universe, begins or ends. Hence nobody is born or dies. Everything is One Implicate Entity enfolded in Chaos which acts to create the illusion of fragmentary entities, which interact in an eternal cycle of recurring events. These events recur in different forms through the continuous changes in conditions. These changes, or continuous state of flux, is another illusion created by the prevalent Force of Chaos. Illusions themselves are Chaotic abstract in action influencing and asserting its dominance as the prevalent whole.

Chapter 8 - <u>Complementary Ideas in Philosophy, Theology and Science</u>

There is no such thing as novelty. There is no such thing as innovation, progress, invention or free will. There is only the Chaotic Intelligence of the Universal Collective Unconscious. This Universal Collective Unconscious (U.C.U.) is every idea, entity and event that ever was and always will be. It (U.C.U.) evolves and devolves, changes form and enacts the illusion of change. Any idea, innovation or invention always existed in the Chaotic Intelligence of the U.C.U. When the U.C.U. evolves to merge with the human species it manifests these already pre-existing forms or archetypes into the illusion of a physical reality. Language is a holistic A-priori entity which is an archetype of the U.C.U. chaotically categorizing everything in terms of metaphoric and explicate entities. Music, art, cinema and literature are counter-chaotic influences within the chaotic whole. They are the Implicate order of the U.C.U. in its highest state of evolution. They are the apex of Human Collective expression. The collage of entities of Chaos expressed in Implicate Fashion. Film, music, art and literature is the U.C.U. reaching its highest expression because it reflects the full evolution and devolution of all entities in the form of the abstract. It is the prevalent abstract expressing itself in the abstract. Music, art, literature and film are chaos expressing itself in holistic, non-fragmentary fashion. All horror, beauty, love, hate, intellect and decadence is expressed in the abstract. Film, literature, music and art epitomize this. They also prove the prevalence of the abstract. Does not T.V., radio, books, theater and art dominate more of our time and psychological conditioning than any other mediums? Are not fictional movies the most watched, influential and most regarded entities in our society, rendering the dominance of the most abstract A-priori entities in the U.C.U., Imagination and creativity?

Further proof of the prevailing existence and dominance of the U.C.U. lies in the complementary ideas and interchangeable concepts that express the Chaotic Whole and holistic Implicate Order. Throughout the history of Philosophy, Theology and Science, there have always been expressions of the unifying prevalent and dominant force. First, in philosophy the whole oneness was expressed by Ancient Eastern philosophies to include Chinese Taoism, India's Hinduism and later Buddhism. Taoism expressed the whole as the Yin-Yang ☯. Hinduism referred to a Cosmic *Egg* from which everything came and was known as Brahma. Both Hinduism and Buddhism refer to the omnipotent Void as the expression of Oneness and the omnipresent Universal force from which all things come from, exist, in and will return to. Theology expressed the theory of a whole universal implicate order force as one God. Examples: Christianity, Islam, and Judaism. Modern era Western Philosophies, particularly the Idealists, also express the U.C.U. and the implicate order. Plato does this in his philosophy of forms, Hegel in his philosophy of Geist or all embracing, omnipresent mind and spirit, the Stoics spoke of the omni-present, all embracing mind-fire as the U.C.U. Implicate Order Force. Schopenhauer described an all powerful Will, in particular the Will to live, as the omnipresent Implicate Order Force. Spinoza cites an interdependent nature as the whole. In science we have the Big Bang Theory expressing everything expanding out of a Singular Whole. We have Einstein's theory of Relativity

$E=MC^2$, wave-particle duality and interchangeability, and finally David Bohm's Implicate order, which implies an eternal metaphysical continuum which I link to Carl Jung's Collective Unconscious. The Scientific theory of Vacuum Genesis coincides with the Void being all prevalent, all creative and omnipresent as is implied theologically in the first lines of Genesis in the Bible and philosophically in Buddhism and Hinduism.

All of these Theological, Philosophical and Scientific citations suggest complementary ideas in history and through all disciplines of study in expressing a whole singular implicate order. This substantiates the existence of a Universal Collective Unconscious that is the omnipresent Cosmic mind and Implicate Order. Every abstract and physical entity chaotically and non-sequentially pre-existed, exists and will always exist in an infinite recurring cycle of events. This flux of events changes form but recurs basically within the same frame of concepts, non-sequentially and chaotically. The chaotic nature of events is evidenced in our dreams and near death experiences, where abstract ideas and visualizations occur randomly and with no set sequence or purpose. This metaphysical explanation of chaos and randomness is supplemented by a

Scientific Physical theory supporting chaos and randomness known as "The Uncertainty Principle" espoused in the 20th Century by Heisenberg. Our realization of an Infinite Chaotic Implicate Order of the U.C.U. with an eternal cycle of explicate entities enfolded within this Implicate U.C.U. is the bedrock and foundation of a Metaphysical Utopian Society which we will now strive to design.

Chapter 9 - <u>Metaphysical Education</u>

The foundation of our Metaphysical Utopian Society will be in its Educational System. The focus of which will be on High School Students and the adult population. The nature of this Education will be passive, participatory and Socratic in nature. It will be designed to Supplement the Current System and Complement it. It is in no way to be mandatory or compulsory. The idea is to introduce philosophy and metaphysics to people as an available concept which is open to all to embrace voluntarily. The goal for the individual is to achieve intellectual stimulation and emotional harmony while feeling interconnected with all other entities, human or otherwise.

At the high school level the education should consist of reading and writing brief book reports. Freshman high school students would read two books and write reports on them. One would be in English Class during the First Semester of the Academic year and the other would be part of their summer reading. During the regular school year they would read the book entitled "The Story of

Philosophy" by Will Durant. They are to be given six months to read and write a brief summary of this book. The summary will include: new words they learned while reading the book, philosophical concepts they became aware of by reading the book and a comparison of how some of the concepts in the book complemented or contradicted their own ideas about metaphysics, theology and philosophy. Prior to the assignment, the teacher would define some terms such as: metaphysics, philosophy, etc. so the student would have a built in basic vocabulary to start with. The students are to be encouraged to look up every word they do not understand in the book, so as to increase and develop their vocabulary. After 3 months a review class will be held to discuss where everyone is at in the book and which words and concepts need to be clarified. This book report, as well as the summer exercise, will be strictly for Extra Credit. Students can be more creative and will enjoy the exercise more if it is not pressurized and compulsory. We want this to be a long term learning experience and not a "get it over with for a grade" experience. The summer reading will consist of the book entitled "The Tao of Physics" by *Fritjof* Capra. This book gives a nice overview to the Eastern religions and compares their complementarity to modern day Scientific theories and Western physics and metaphysics. A brief summary by each student will be submitted at the start of their Sophomore year followed by discussion. During the H.S. Sophomore year students will read "The Holographic Universe" by Michael Talbot. The same 6 month book report exercise will ensue as the year before. By this time students will have a good metaphysical foundation and reference source in these 3 books. These exercises will also aid students in developing reading, writing and vocabulary skills. "The Story of Philosophy" by Will Durant is also an excellent learning tool for history as it carries one thru the ancient western and modern philosophies. The Tao of Physics gives an excellent account of Eastern Theologies and philosophies and also gives a comparison of Complementary ideas in physics and metaphysics. More analysis of complementary ideas in physics and metaphysics appears in "The Holographic Universe." This book also delves into comparisons in physics and Neurobiology. The modern concept of David Bohm's Implicate order is explored in this book as well as a comprehensive discussion of philosophies, and actual experiments and experiences such as Near Death

Experiences, and Dream analysis. Hence, these 3 books and the discussions they generate will not only involve metaphysical thought but will also enhance students knowledge in reading, writing, vocabulary, history, philosophy and science. The students opinion and summaries of these books will also aid them in enhancing their critical thinking and writing skills.

Adult Education should follow several model home study and New School Curriculums already in existence. The University of Metaphysics is one such home study curriculum that performs the function of giving the individual a broad range of metaphysical concepts from which to formulate his or her own metaphysical thesis. The intellectual, spiritual and emotional stimulation which Doctor Masters curriculum and metaphysical ministry provides is something every individual should experience as a young or older adult. It is the culmination of a persons strife to become one with the Collective Universal mind or the Collective Unconscious.

Other books which are extremely insightful and easy to read include: "Lao Tzu - Chung Te Tao" which explains the philosophy of Taoism, and "Meditations" by Marcus Aurelius, which also provides some intriguing metaphysical and common sense lessons.

Books which address a practical application of metaphysical concepts in Society include "It Takes a Village" by Hillary Rodham Clinton and the classic "Utopia" by Sir Thomas More. These books would serve as excellent supplemental and extra credit material to 3rd and 4th year high school students.

Another great model for metaphysical and philosophical adult education exists at the "New School" located in the Village Section of Manhattan, New York City. Here, there are numerous philosophy courses and science courses that deal with metaphysical concepts. One such course is entitled "The Intelligent Universe" which deals with Cosmic Evolution, Philosophical and metaphysical history, as well as current cosmological and philosophical ideas. Complementary ideas in science, philosophy, theology and history are explored as well as such big picture questions like "Is the universe one whole living organism?", "Is there a cosmic mind which is omnipresent and contains the universe and all of its entities encapsulated in it?" These are among the most important questions one may ponder and are the reasons why metaphysics and philosophy are the most important subjects humanity can delve into. This is why it is incumbent upon us in the metaphysical community to export philosophical and metaphysical concepts and discussions in our schools and communities. These discussions will also unite communities towards other endeavors such as charitable causes and community safety because metaphysical discussions tend to emphasize oneness, wholeness and the interconnectedness of all humanity and nature.

A final idea concerning metaphysical education would be to combine all of the aforementioned ideas and institute an elective course for senior high school and/or adults. The course would be titled "Complementary Ideas and Interchangeable Concepts in Physics and Metaphysics." This course would cover all of the readings mentioned previously: "The Story of Philosophy", "The Tao of Physics" and "The Holographic Universe." Comparisons would be made using these books, world history, theology, mythology, and current day physics and cosmology. The interconnectedness and interchangeable concepts of all these disciplines would be discussed and critically analyzed. Book reports and comparative essays would constitute a major portion of the homestudy program part of the course while broad discussions on complementary issues involving metaphysics , physics and society would take place in the classroom. Practical application of metaphysical concepts in our global society would also be discussed during the course.

An example of a complementary idea with metaphysical implications is that of the correlation between Quantum physics and consciousness. In physics the Casimir effect, confirmed in January 1997, indicated that the interaction of a Vacuum causes a 20 nanometer separation between Intermolecular Bonds. This is the same amount of spacing separating synapses in neurons. Hence we have a correlation of Vacuum forces in two different disciplines, physics and neurobiology. The term "Vacuum" itself can be correlated to the "Void" which is spoken about in Christianity, Buddhism, Hinduism and Taoism. Hence this comparison of the Casimir Effect and Snynaptic spacing lends itself to metaphysical and mystical correlation. The physical sciences complement metaphysical concepts and visa-versa.

David Bohm's theory of "Wholeness and the Implicate Order" is another excellent example of the interconnectedness of the physical and metaphysical. Bohm's concept of totality included both mind and matter.

In a 1989 interview at the Nils Bohr Institute in Copenhagen, Bohm mentioned the dangers we face as a society and the changes we will have to make in our thinking to have a future. He indicates that we need a more holistic approach to the ecological problem and <u>must</u> find something else in life besides economic growth; if it continues unchecked, it will destroy the planet. The emerging change in consciousness is the challenge and the key. Our future depends on whether we feel like part of this whole or whether we feel separate. In his book "Wholeness and the Implicate Order" as well as in Michael Talbot's book on "The Holographic Universe" Bohm states that, as in a Hologram, "any element contains enfolded within itself the totality of its Universe." [Talbot, 1991] Although Bohm's theory is modern with scientific backing, it is an overall metaphysical explanation for the whole. His 20th Century metaphysics, correlates with the stoic philosophy of 400 B.C. Stoic physicists taught that the primordial source of being in all its forms is a certain substance, omnipresent in the universe, which can best be described as mind. Mind was held to consist of a real and positive stuff, though it is the thinnest and most impalpable kind imaginable. This mind-fire which possessed consciousness and purpose and will, was both creator and the material of the Universe; it took shape in innumerable different manifestations thereby giving all things their particular substances and forms, and producing out of itself the visible world and all within it.

Marcus Aurelius, the famous philosopher-Emperor of the Roman Empire, accentuates this mind-fire concept of the stoics when he dwells on its operations upon the Universe as a whole. He may call it God, Zeus, Nature, Providence, Fate, Necessity or Law. Marcus Aurelius and the stoics expression of the whole correlates with Bohm's Implicate Order as well as other metaphysical expressions of the whole to include: Hegel's Geist, the Hindus & Buddhists Void, God, Carl Jung's Collective Unconscious. These correlations exist because, as mentioned previously, all these concepts always existed and always will exist. Only the manifestations change in an eternal cyclical flux. This is the metaphysical concept of the universal collective unconscious (U.C.U.) in action.

Another correlation of physics and Eastern mysticism is illustrated in "The Tao of Physics." Here the comparison of the "physical vacuum" and the Void of Eastern Mysticism is made. The physical vacuum - as it is called in the quantum field theory - is not a state of nothingness, but contains the potentiality for all forms of the particular world. These forms, in turn, are not independent physical entities but merely transient manifestations of the Underlying Void. As the Sutra says "Form is emptiness and emptiness is indeed form." [Capra, 1991:207-223]

The relation between the virtual particles and the vacuum is an essential dynamic relation; the vacuum is truly a living void pulsating in endless rhythms of creation and destruction. The discovery of the dynamic quality of the vacuum is seen by many physicists as one of the most important findings of modern physics. From its role as an empty container of the physical phenomena, the void has emerged as a dynamic quantity of utmost importance. The results of modern physics thus seem to confirm the words of the Chinese Sage Chuang Tzu: "When one knows that the great void is full of Chi, one realizes that there is no such thing as nothingness.

The "endless rhythms of creation and destruction" reflect the infinite chaotic cycle of all entities while the parallels of the mystical void and scientific vacuum serve as another example of an unconscious coincidence further substantiating the existence of an omnipresent Universal

Collective Unconscious or Universal mind being all prevalent, chaotic and eternal. [Capra, 1991:223] We all exist as reflections of this Universal mind, as part of this Universal mind, and as this Universal mind realizing itself, first unconsciously and eventually consciously.

Plato's Republic and St. Thomas More's Utopia were compulsory. We need to constantly introduce and inform, not dictate. Our Utopia is a state of mind and awareness and not the state or state imposed. The philosopher-King Plato speaks of in his Republic can be all of us. Education should be an awareness experience not a competition or a discriminator. Compulsion, imposition, competition and aggression need to be subtly phased out. Cooperation, non-compulsory and passive education, intellectualization, and awareness of our link with the omnipresent Universal mind needs to become our first collective priority with material wealth only pursued for basic subsistence needs and not as a lifelong quest. Self-aggrandizement and individual ambition also need to be phased out of our psyche. We are already unconsciously evolving towards oneness and collective Universal self-awareness through our complex information systems, i.e., Books, T.V., internet, telecommunications, transportation and all technological advances that have brought people and information closer together and more accessible. The Implicate Order and Wholeness is also expressed unconsciously through our economic system which uses centralized currency as opposed to a barter system. Centralized Governments also express an unconscious evolution towards Universal oneness and U.C.U. self awareness. The evolution of the Nation State is an unconscious replica of the Universal Implicate Order, Universal Mind or U.C.U.

Organizations like the University of Metaphysics (UOM) and Oversoul ministry need to join forces and expand to propagate metaphysical education and humanitarian actions. Our economy and society must be based on these two principals in order for us to reach the height of our evolution which is the collective conscious awareness of our oneness with the Implicate Order of the Universal Mind. Then the U.C.U. will become the U.C.C. Universal Collective Conscious.

Chaos will be one with Cosmos. Energy one with entropy, consciousness one with the unconscious. Past one with future, senses one with concepts, abstract one with physical. Yin one with Yang. Metaphysical one with empirical physical science. Void one with matter. This already is the case, all that is needed is for all of us to consciously realize this Implicate order of Universal mind for the Collective United bliss and awareness to evolve and prevail. Living and thinking metaphysically will achieve this apex of our evolution. As Dr. Paul Leon Masters, the dean of the University of Metaphysics (UOM) and the founder of the International Metaphysics ministry (IMM) says:

> "Truly, if all the world has metaphysical knowledge, and then lived by it, indeed, all the problems of the earth would be solved, and peace, love, harmony, and prosperity would be the experience of all humankind. For this reason metaphysics is so important for each individual and for society collectively. It is by gaining such knowledge through psychic-mystical means that the

world's understanding of itself can be accelerated beyond the slow pace of the empirical scientists."

Unconsciously coincidental, Dr. Masters Metaphysical Paradise parallels the "Taoist Utopia" proclaimed by Lao Tzu and Chuang Tzu in their description of the Tao paradise:

"The men of old, while the chaotic condition was yet undeveloped shared the placid tranquility which belonged to the whole world. At that time yin and yang were harmonious and still; their resting and movement proceeded without any disturbance; the four seasons had their definite times; not a single thing received any injury, and no living being came to a premature end. Men might be possessed of the faculty of knowledge, but they has no occasion for its use. This was what is called the state of perfect unity. At this time, there was no action on the part of anyone - but a constant manifestation of spontaneity."

This Taoist ideal is directly parallel to the Metaphysical Ideal Dr. Masters speaks of. The Taoist Ideal cites the harmony of the yin and the yang. Dr. Masters cites the potential harmony of Metaphysical ideals with empirical science in the following statement from the UOM course material:

".... Indeed much metaphysical knowledge may be in contradiction to what 'appears to be' to empirical scientists. Ultimately, the two will be in harmony with one another as humankind evolves to the point where outer science discovers that the farthest reaches of infinity, or outer space, are one and the same as the inner infinite depths of the human mind."

This metaphysical ideal will become a reality when the Unconscious Coincidences mentioned previously in this thesis become conscious realizations and actualizations embedded in the human mind. This means that...

"…. each of us, as part of the One Life of the Universe share a Co-Ownership with EVERYTHING that is. The realization of this truth creates a mental atmosphere. … which aids in the acceptance within the individual mind that prosperity or 'having' or 'owning' is the natural course of Universal Life individualized as the human being."

This state of mind whereby we individually and collectively realize our minds as one with the Infinite Universal mind will be the evolution to the metaphysical Utopia which is the Universal mind realizing itself. The human species is the manifestation of this realization. The human mind is the Universal mind realizing itself. It is also infinite and chaotically recurring. Our conscious recognition of this is our eternal bliss.

I do not want to be known as an innovator because if you believe, as I do, in a UCU there is no innovation only discovery and awareness of what always has been in the Universal mind. I would only want to be known as someone who became aware of the dominance of the abstract and the implicate order of the U.C.U. Universal mind and who helped others to become exposed to this intellectual bliss and awareness. Also, that in this self-education and collective metaphysical education, people's lives became happier, less stressed, enriched and enlightened, prolonged and safe. Focus on abstract i.e. reading philosophy and metaphysics both modern and ancient. The Oxford Companion to Philosophy is an excellent reference in addition to Dr. Masters UOM course material, the Tao of Physics by Fritjof Capra and the Holographic Universe by Michael Talbot. Reading, studying, understanding and discussing these materials and putting your own thoughts towards developing your own metaphysical thesis is the most enriching intellectual and emotional experience you can have. As Dr. Masters says, if we all thought and lived metaphysically, there would be no problems only collective peace and harmony. We would truly evolve to become aware of our co-ownership with the Universal mind or UCU. Numerous Hopi or Ascetic like small metaphysical communities like UOM. - IMM studying and exchanging metaphysical ideas while supporting charitable and collective humanitarian actions and sharing and equally distributing economic resources voluntarily among communities or groups. As Hillary Clinton says "It takes a village". In this spirit of Community we can all live better, and develop intellectually towards individual and collective bliss and emotional harmony. Such metaphysical communities, societies or groups would serve as a global paradigm for a Universal metaphysical Utopian Society. Lets expedite our evolution by providing this model now. Metaphysical intellectualization, charity, volunteerism, cooperation and appropriate sharing of economic and subsistence resources.

Social and community services should dominate economic market of jobs and services. Teachers, youth counselors, and social workers should be compensated better with more job slots made available to care for the millions of disabled and displaced children as well as the chronically ill people, both mentally and physically. Community and charity service must be constantly encouraged because it manifests our interconnectedness with each other and the U.C.U.

Chapter 10 - The Explicate World as Allegory and Representation of the Implicate U.C.U.

Every explicate entity is an allegorical manifestation of the infinite, implicate, chaotic, spontaneous and cyclical U.C.U. This statement is in itself an allegorical representation that unconsciously coincides with numerous other abstract explicate entities and theories that I will now begin to list.

One such allegorical representation can be found in the Christian belief of three Gods in one. The three explicate Gods of the Father, Son and the Holy Spirit all make up one God and all are interchangeable with the implicate Omnipotent and Omnipresent God. An unconscious allegorical coincidence and comparison to this would be the concept of the spectrum of light containing all of the various colors which make up white light. Red, blue and yellow are the basic explicate colors that make up the implicate white light. Is this not a reflection and manifestation of the theological trinity concept? Is not a traffic light made up of three colors (red, yellow and green). Another allegorical connection is the wave particle duality. A wave and a particle are categorized by science as being interchangeable and as the same entity manifested in either form. Here both the wave and the particle are both explicate and implicate at the same time.

I will now cite examples and allegories of the dominance of the abstract and mankind's acknowledgement of such. Dark matter makes up more than 99% of the universe according to empirical scientists. Dark matter is also the most abstract, chaotic and entropic physical entity categorized by science. Yet it is considered the most powerful gravitational source in the galaxies. The same is said of black holes which are gravitational voids in space that suck up all matter and energy on its horizon. This is also considered the most powerful force in the universe. How convenient it is that the most powerful physical forces in the universe are categorized and related to the concept of the Void. Does not Hinduism, Buddhism and Taoism cite the Void as the all powerful and prevalent formless nothingness from which everything comes from and will return? Does not the Christian Bible refer to the world being "Void" at the beginning of creation in the first lines of the Book of Genesis? Another allegorical indication of the prevalence and dominance of the abstract, chaotic, entropic and infinite Void can be found in the practice of meditation. In meditation we seek to empty of minds of all conscious thought. This is said to be tranquil, pleasant and relaxing. Is this not our unconscious attempt to merge with the U.C.U. by making our explicate conscious brain void in order to merge with the void of the U.C.U. It is a "Void on Void" so to speak. This merging with the U.C.U. is also manifested in our dreams and in near death experiences. Logically when we die our explicate conscious mind in our physical brain merely goes back to its implicate home which is the infinite, chaotic, abstract and cyclical U.C.U.

More examples of abstract dominance. The smallest organic organisms on earth take the form of bacteria and viruses. We have no indication that these organisms contain any sophisticated form of consciousness or purpose. We can logically assume them to be spontaneous, chaotic and unconscious. Yet these organisms are acknowledged by humanity and empirical science as being the first living organisms on earth. They were here before us and they will be here after us. One way or the other we all eventually succumb to some form of bacteria or virus in the manifestation of diseases. Hence, the smallest and perhaps the most chaotically unconscious living organism categorized by man is also the most prevalent and dominant species on earth. This is another allegorical irony that substantiates the prevalence of the abstract over the physical. Water initially appears as a weak, wishy-washy substance. Yet it is the source of all life. Water makes up over 90% of the human body. No organic entity, plant, animal or otherwise can exist without water. Humanity has even harnessed the immense power of water to generate electricity via powerful dams and falls. Water is also allegorical to the philosophical concept of the eternal flux. Water flows and is indicative of what the Taoists call "The Way of Nature." Heraclitus and Buddha also cite the flux as prevalent in their philosophies.

The dominance of A-priori abstractions and their spontaneous and chaotic manifestations are obvious. The idea of "love at first sight" is not deductible or logical. It is an A-priori phenomena and its roots can only be linked to the U.C.U. It is an abstract emotion that dominates us in a whimsical and chaotic manner. When one is struck by this abstract emotion of love as with hate nothing physical, logical, organized or civilized can stand up to this A-priori phenomena. Music is also an abstract A-priori phenomena with its roots in the U.C.U. Its spontaneous and chaotic will manifests itself to resonate with the human mind. This has made music as well as other abstract forms of art such as cinema and television the underlying dominant force in our present civilization. There are numerous examples of this. The rock music of the sixties in the U.S. incited anti-war protests and created countercultures among the youth. Today's rap music inspires rebellion and even violence among today's youth. The Voodoo drum rhythms inspired revolution among the slaves of Haiti in the early 1800s. It had such a powerful impact on the revolting slaves that they overcame impossible odds to overthrow the numerically superior and better equipped French army. All of these examples demonstrate the superiority of an A-priori abstract force (as in the case of music) resonating with the human mind to overcome physical reality.

The prevalence of the abstract can be seen in today's society. More and more of peoples time is spent in the abstract. This is because we are evolving unconsciously back to our A-priori roots which are in the implicate, infinite, and chaotic UCU. Let's think about it for a minute. We spend an average of eight hours a day sleeping and dreaming. Most people have at least two hours round-trip of commuting each day to and from work where they are most likely listening to music, news, or talk shows on the radio. Tack on another two to three hours for television, movies, and spectator sports and you wind up with a day of thirteen hours spent as an abstract observer.

Man created the computer as a replication of himself. The computer needs input from man just as man gets his input from the UCU. The concept of the internet is man unconsciously acknowledging the interconnectedness of all explicate entities that comprise the implicate UCU. Man is unconsciously creating a metaphysical utopia via the allegory of the internet. Here we see the unavoidable fact that the Ideal is always superior to the physical explicate reality. Is not the fantasy perceived always better than the fantasy realized or enacted? Our yearning love is always more stimulating than love realized. Our image of someone we idolize is always more beautiful, tantalizing and satisfying than what that person really is. The truth of the matter is that the abstract Ideal is the permanent, eternal, implicate reality and the physical reality of life is just a temporary illusion and an allegory or archetype manifested in the explicate order to merely symbolize and reflect the implicate UCU. In this context our dream world is closer to reality than the world we physically live in. Death is merely a transformation from the explicate consciousness to the implicate, enfolded, chaotic infinity of the UCU. It is the dream world extending itself and remaining merged with the UCU. In other words, it is our consciousness returning to the implicate chaotic, holistic unconsciousness which is one and infinite.

Some more explicate allegories that replicate and unconsciously connect us to the implicate UCU. The concept of encapsulation. This can be seen in the potency that drugs have inside of a small capsule. Is this not a replica of the Big Bang energy exploding out of a dense singularity. The atom itself is also an allegory of encapsulation. There is also a viewpoint which states that the entire universe is really one, implicate, encapsulated mind with all explicate entities reflecting this. Another allegory that connects past, present and future into one cyclical, infinite time can be found in our penchant and interest in history. This connection between the explicate entities of past, present and future to implicate cyclical and holistic time can also be found in the expression "light year". The term light year denotes the distance a far away celestial object is from our observation. The object is so far away that we can only measure its distance from us in terms of the time it takes for light to reach us, hence the term light year. This means that if something is one thousand light years away we are looking at it as it was one thousand years ago. This conceptualization of the "light year" is mankind's and the UCU's unconscious acknowledgement of past and present being the same in infinite cyclical time.

One last analogy depicts the universe as a stream. The stream is the implicate flow and the waves, ice, forks and sediment in the stream are explicate entities which can only exist as interrelated parts of the implicate flux that is the stream of water. Hence, all explicate entities (abstract and physical) are composed of the implicate chaotic and abstract UCU and also reflect this infinite UCU.

Chapter 11 - <u>Living the Utopia</u>

Chaos and entropy are dominant and will always manifest themselves one way or the other. Chaos cannot be suppressed or destroyed in the temporal physical world. This will only exacerbate chaos and create more chaos. Chaos and entropy can only be channeled into the abstract. Our only hope is to allow chaos to flow its course in the abstract, via music, fictional horror movies, etc. You can only balance an abstract force (chaos) with an abstract channel (music, fiction, film, imaginative literature, etc.). We must strive to trivialize hierarchy, competition, labeling and categorizing. We must stress and emphasize cooperation, charity, teaching, selfless social work, metaphysical intellectualization and pacification. Emptying our minds and giving of ourselves always makes us feel better. This is because we are unconsciously merging with our implicate, abstract UCU roots. This is also why listening to music, watching T.V. , meditating, dreaming and engaging in reverie are our most pleasant experiences.

These experiences are where we merge our conscious minds with the implicate abstract and chaotic universal mind or UCU. If we can consciously realize this then and only then can we reach the height of our evolution which is the metaphysical utopia and ultimate bliss. Realizing and flowing with the abstract creates pacification. If only one explicate mind recognizes itself as one with the implicate UCU, this represents more of reality then billions of conscious minds ignoring or not being aware of the implicate abstract UCU. Remember over 99% of the universe is implicate, chaotic and abstract. Therefore, the billions of conscious minds are only a tiny fraction of reality. The only real reality is the implicate reality of the UCU and when we become aware of this we merge with the implicate abstract UCU and reach the metaphysical utopia. Let us reach the ultimate bliss and teach this awareness to others thereby completing the full cycle of the Universal Mind or UCU realizing itself through all its explicate entities. Metaphysical intellectualization will naturally flow into humanitarianism and communitarianism because the metaphysical abstract naturally dominates over the physical explicate reality. The implicate metaphysical UCU merges all conscious and unconscious explicate entities and this is why reaching UCU self-awareness naturally creates a collective psyche of pacification and universal oneness. This collective psyche of pacification and universal oneness and UCU self-awareness at any level with any explicate, conscious or unconscious entity is the metaphysical utopia.

Bibliography

Bercholz, Samuel 1993
Entering the Stream. Boston, Massachusetts
Shambhala Publications, Inc.

Berrill, N.J. 1957
Man' Emerging Mind. New York, N.Y.
Premier Books, Fawcett World Library

Capra, Fritjof 1991
The Tao of Physics. Boston, Massachusetts
Shambhala Publications, Inc.

Dennett, Daniel C. 1991
Consciousness Explained. Canada
Little, Brown & Company

Durant, Will 1961

The Story of Philosophy. New York, N.Y.

Washington Square Press

Gleick, James 1987

Chaos. Ontario, Canada

Penguin Books

Hawkins, Stephen 1988

A Brief History of Time. New York, N.Y.

Bantam Books

Honderich, Ted 1995

The Oxford Companion to Philosophy. Oxford, N.Y.

Oxford University Press, Inc.

Madsen, Per 1997

"The Martinus Cosmology," <u>Venture Inward.</u> july):34-39

Masters, Paul Leon 1997

"University of Metaphysics Course Material"

Sagan, Carl 1980

<u>Cosmos</u>. New York, N.Y.

Carl Sagan Production, Inc.

Schlipp, Paul Arthur 1970

<u>Albert Einstein: Philosopher - Scientist</u>.

Peru, Illinois

Open Court Publishing Company

Schopenhauer, Arthur 1819

The World as Will and Representation. Volume I

New York, N.Y.

Dover Publications Inc.

Talbot, Michael 1991

The Holographic Universe. New York, N.Y.

Harper Collins Publisher, Inc.

Tipler, Frank J. 1994

The Physics of Immortality. New York, NY

Doubleday Publishing Inc.

Wolf, Fred Alan 1996

The Spiritual Universe. New York, N.Y.

Simon & Schuster, Inc.

Zukav, Gary 1979

<u>The Dancing Wu Li Masters.</u> New York, N.Y.

Bantam Books

About the Author

My name is Vincent J. Leardi. I am currently employed as a Special Education and World History teacher. I reside in Staten Island, New York with my family. I served in the U. S. military as an Army Captain from 1984 – 1990. I have a BS degree in Engineering and a minor in International Relations from the U. S. Military Academy at West Point. I also have a masters degree in Business Administration from Boston University.

My penchant and love for philosophy and metaphysics inspired me to write this book. I hope you enjoy reading it as much as I have enjoyed writing it.

www.ingramcontent.com/pod-product-compliance
Lightning Source LLC
Chambersburg PA
CBHW050359290526
45786CB00003B/1051